MW00935972

RENAL DIET
& COOKBOOK

Your Complete Guide to the Renal Diet with Over
30 Easy and Delicious Kidney Friendly Recipes

Disclaimer

The information in this book is not to be used as medical advice. The recipes should be used in combination with guidance from your physician. Please consult your physician before beginning any diet. It is especially important for those with diabetes, and those on medications to consult with their physician before making changes to their diet.

Disclaimer and Terms of Use: Effort has been made to ensure that the information in this book is accurate and complete, however, the author and the publisher do not warrant the accuracy of the information, text and graphics contained within the book due to the rapidly changing nature of science, research, known and unknown facts and internet. The Author and the publisher do not hold any responsibility for errors, omissions or contrary interpretation of the subject matter herein. This book is presented solely for motivational and informational purposes only.

Table of Contents

Introduction

Your kidneys are two of the most important organs in your body. These little powerhouses are responsible for filtering and removing waste from your body. Given the fact that some people can have a kidney removed and do just fine without it, the kidneys have been given a reputation of not being that important. Between knowing that you can live a normal healthy life with just one kidney, and improvements in medical technology, such as medications and dialysis, that improve the quality of life for people with late stage kidney disease, the importance of maintaining kidney health seems to have become less of a priority. It really doesn't matter if you are reading this because you have been coping with kidney disease for years, or because your doctor has suggested a renal diet plan or even if you are taking preventative measures to maintain kidney health into the future, placing an emphasis on protecting and healing your kidneys means an improved quality of life and better health now and for years to come.

The kidneys are located towards your back in the abdominal area, with one placed on each side of your spinal column. The kidney's function is to purify the blood by removing waste products, maintain the proper amount of fluids in the body, and balance the concentrations of electrolytes in your system. Think for a moment about all of the toxins that you encounter on any given day. They can come from environmental sources and also the foods that you eat. Even those of us with the cleanest diets are still susceptible to overloading our kidneys. With kidneys that are functioning normally, these stressors are generally not an issue. However, when it occurs that the kidneys are not able to function properly, they are no longer able to remove the waste from your body in an effective manner. This means that those toxins build up and basically put additional stress on all of the other systems in your body. This reaction is what we call renal failure and it is the main concern behind the development of the renal diet.

There are certain nutrients that are broken down and processed by the kidneys. When the kidneys have reduced function, these nutrients can accumulate in your body and cause some potentially serious issues. When you are eating a renal diet to protect your kidney health, you will want to be watchful of the big four: Protein, Phosphorus, Calcium and Potassium. Learning which foods are high in these nutrients and which ones are acceptable for your new dietary lifestyle will require some education, but it is not something that is unrealistic for you to handle. In fact, once you become accustomed to the renal diet, what once felt like restrictive choices will feel like a dietary lifestyle that is filled with endless options and fresh, wholesome flavors. Eating to heal and protect your kidneys is as much about preparing yourself mentally as it is about preparing the dishes suggested in this book. Keep the mindset that this is not overcomplicated, completely within your reach and an interesting new opportunity and you will find that it is actually quite easy to adopt the renal diet lifestyle.

What is Renal Failure?

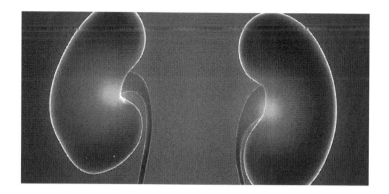

In the simplest of terms, renal failure is when your kidney stop removing the waste products from your system as effectively as they once did. There are various causes behind renal failure and different stages of kidney disease as well.

Causes

Renal failure can occur from a preexisting condition that stresses the kidneys, referred to as chronic renal failure, or from an injury to both kidneys, which is referred to as acute renal failure. Acute renal failure can be the result of an unexpected trauma to the kidneys such as an automobile accident, a serious fall or an illness in which severe dehydration has occurred. To suffer from acute renal failure, both kidneys must be compromised. If only one kidney is damaged, the other one will step up and compensate for the reduce function.

In preexisting conditions, renal failure is something different. In these situations it is almost always the case that both kidneys become damaged as a result of the underlying cause. Some common causes of chronic renal failure include poorly controlled diabetes, severely high blood pressure, chronic glomerulonephritis and occasionally kidney stones or prostate disease. The human body is a complicated system and this basic list does not begin to cover all of the different conditions that can in some way contribute to the reduced function of the kidneys.

Symptoms

It is quite common that early renal failure does not cause any noticeable symptoms. For this reason, if you have any underlying condition that could potentially affect your kidneys it is very important that you see your doctor on a regular basis so that they can monitor your kidney function and catch reduced renal function early before it poses any life threatening risks. Once renal failure has reached the point where you begin to notice symptoms, the first ones that you are likely to notice include:

- Lethargy
- Weakness
- Fatigue
- Loss of Appetite
- Shortness of Breath
- Swelling

The more serious symptoms of renal failure that need to be addressed immediately include:

- High Blood Potassium
- Elevated Urea Levels in the Blood
- Metabolic Acidosis
- Arrhythmias
- Congested Heart Disease

Treatments

Depending on the stage of your kidney disease, there are options available for treatment. Those options include prevention, diet, medications and dialysis. To determine the best options for your condition, you are going to want to discuss the choices with your doctor and follow through on any suggested or prescribed regimen. If you are in the early stages of compromised kidney function, an ounce of prevention is worth a lifetime of health. If you are suffering from any of the conditions that put additional stress on your kidneys, such as high blood pressure or diabetes, take control of the disease and do what you can to reduce its presence in your life and the effects on your body.

This book focuses on the dietary lifestyle that is important for kidney health. You will notice that this diet is also great for people that have preexisting diabetes or high blood pressure, as it is low in added sugars and sodium. A renal diet is a holistic approach to treating various degrees of renal failure. If your disease has reached the stage where you are considering, or currently undergoing, dialysis, you will need to speak with your medical care provider about the ways that your diet should be amended. Dialysis helps to remove all of the impurities from your blood, so in most cases in is not only unnecessary to be restrictive, but you might also need to eat additional amounts of typically limited foods to replace the nutrients that have been removed from your body.

Now, with the technicalities out of the way, let's begin to focus on the next 30 days of your life that are going to be filled with kidney friendly, delicious and nourishing foods.

Following a Renal Diet

The point of a renal diet is to reduce the stress on your kidneys by reducing the amount of waste products your body is forced to produce. There are certain foods, and nutrients that are more stressful for the kidneys, causing them to work harder. These are the exact foods that you are looking to eliminate from your diet. Most people that have been advised to follow a renal diet must pay close attention to their daily intake levels of protein, phosphorus, potassium, calcium and sodium. You likely recognize protein, calcium and sodium and the idea of limiting all of those foods sounds daunting.

Keep in mind that you also need to keep track of phosphorus and potassium and suddenly meeting your unique dietary needs has become overwhelming. Keeping your kidneys as stress free and healthy as possible might take discipline and focused attention on what you eat, but the last thing that you need to feel is that it is simply too difficult and unrealistic. Here, we outline the basics of the renal diet for you, along with a comprehensive list of what foods you can have and which ones should be avoided. Here, within just a few pages is everything you need to know about the renal diet.

Key Nutrients and Kidney Health

As you settle into the renal diet, the two biggest components of your diet that you need to be aware of are protein and phosphorus. These two alone put added stress on your kidneys. Depending on your condition, you may also be advised to reduce the levels of calcium, potassium and sodium in your diet as well. This dietary plan has been formulated to offer you nutritious choices that are low in protein and phosphorus. We have also reduced the amounts of calcium, potassium and sodium. It is a good idea to discuss your unique dietary needs with your physician or a licensed nutritionist to determine if you need to further reduce your daily intake of any of these nutrients.

Protein:

Approximately 75 percent of your body is made of protein. It is absolutely essential for vitally physiological functions. The right amount of protein helps to keep you energized, balances the acid/base relationships in your body, produces antibodies and hormones, and plays an important part in wound healing and tissue repair. When you eat protein, it produces waste that must be filtered through your kidneys. Generally, this isn't a problem, but there are two factors that come into play that make it more of an issue. The first is that as a society, we eat much more protein that is necessary for our bodies to function. This overconsumption puts undue stress on the kidneys. Secondly, the waste filtration process of protein can be difficult for people with compromised kidneys. If you are able to limit your protein intake to a level that satisfies your body's requirements without over indulging, then you help reduce the stress on your kidneys.

The question then becomes just how much protein should you consume in a day. For the average person, about 0.8 g of protein per kilogram of body weight meets the requirement. If you have compromised kidney function, you should reduce that amount slightly to 0.7-0.75 g of protein per kilogram of body weight. If you are suffering from more advanced kidney disease, or have been instructed to severely restrict protein intake, this number may be lower.

One kilogram is approximately 2.2 lbs. If you weigh 150 lbs, that is about 68 kg. An average person, consuming 0.8 g of protein per kg would need about 54 g of protein per day. Someone with compromised kidney function would need about 47 to 51 g of protein, or less depending on their individual condition. For reference, one 4 ounce chicken breast has approximately 35 g of protein and a half cup of cottage cheese has 15 g of protein. As you can see, it can be quite easy to consume above the recommended guidelines. Because protein is essential, and satisfying, it is recommended that you break up your protein consumption over the course of the day. This will help ease the stress on your kidneys as well.

One thing that many people who begin eating a renal diet have trouble adjusting to is the small amounts of protein. When you are accustomed to a quarter pound, or more burger, the idea of consuming just one to two ounces of protein at a meal can make you feel deprived. This feeling can be escalated when you take into consideration that you also have to be aware of phosphorus, potassium, calcium and sodium. There is no need to despair. There are plenty of delicious foods that you can choose to satisfy protein needs while still staying within the guidelines of your renal plan. For the most part, you just need to reduce the amount of protein consumed while looking out mainly for phosphorous. Egg whites are pure albumin and are the best protein for you. Two egg whites contain approximately 7 g of protein. Additionally, fatty fish such as salmon, mackerel, tuna and trout, along with lean meats are some of the best protein options.

Phosphorus:

Phosphorus is a mineral that plays a huge role in keeping your bones healthy. While a certain amount of phosphorus is important for your health, too much phosphorus in your body can cause some serious issues, such as calcium deposits in your lungs, heart and eyes. Excess phosphorus can also actually pull calcium stores from your bones, causing them to become extremely frail and weak. Most of the time, the body has a very good system for keeping phosphorus in proper balance. The kidneys work to pull all of the extra phosphorus out of your blood system, eliminating the possibility of dangerous phosphorus overload. When you are suffering from compromised kidney function, your kidneys are not able to process the amount of phosphorus that they were once able to. For this reason, it is recommended that people who are following a renal diet should take careful note of how much phosphorus they consume on a daily basis.

Phosphorus can be naturally occurring in foods, or it can be chemically added. Many processed beverages such as beer, dark sodas, chocolate drinks and dairy drinks are very high in phosphorus. Additionally, many dairy products, organ meats and processed foods are high in phosphorus. When looking at nutritional labels, you will want to look for phosphorus listed as PHOS, Dicalcium phosphate, Disodium phosphate, Monosodium phosphate, Phosphoric acid, Sodium hexameta-phosphate, Trisodium phosphate, Sodium tripolyphosphate and Tetrasodium pyrophosphate. Most people will want to keep their phosphorus level somewhere between 2.5 and 4.5 mg/dL. However, as with all things, you should have a discussion with your health care provider to determine the appropriate level of phosphorus for your body and your condition.

Being on the renal diet does not mean that you cannot have any phosphorus, it simply means that you have to be very cautious and choose wisely when it comes to food sources that contain phosphorus. You should always aim for lower phosphorus foods that offer high nutritive content rather than smaller amounts of non nutritious high phosphorus foods.

Calcium:

Calcium is another mineral that is vital for bone health. Almost all of the calcium in your body can be found in your bones and teeth. In a normally functioning body, calcium is absorbed into your body by supplements and the foods you eat at the same rate at which it is excreted. In other words, there is a perfect balance, with no excess or deficit. This balance can be thrown out of whack in cases of kidney disease. Many people with kidney disease have trouble maintaining balanced calcium stores. This issue becomes even more complicated when you realize that people with compromised kidney function suffer from both calcium deficiencies and calcium overload. Both of these unbalanced states can pose serious threats to your health. Not enough calcium means your bones will become brittle, predisposing you to catastrophic injuries from even the littlest accidents. Too much calcium puts you at risk of developing dangerous calcium deposits in your vital organs. So, what are you to do? The answer is to first speak with your doctor.

When you have limited kidney function, it is important to have your blood calcium levels monitored on a regular basis. If you are suffering from low calcium levels, you might be prescribed a supplement. If your calcium levels are too high, dietary changes will be discussed with you. You should speak with your physician or nutritionist in regards to how much calcium you should be consuming daily and what the best food sources of calcium are. The problem with many traditional calcium containing foods, such as dairy products, is that those foods are also typically high in phosphorus, which must be closely monitored with impaired kidney function. If you have been told to limit calcium, make sure to stay away from traditional calcium containing foods, and also those that have fortified or are enriched to contain added calcium. As part of the renal diet, it is important to look at every food label to make sure that none of the ingredients could potentially harm your condition.

Potassium:

Potassium is a nutrient that is vital for many physiological functions. When in proper balance, potassium helps to regulate your heart beat, maintains appropriate electrolyte and fluid balance and plays a major role in how well muscles and nerves function. Potassium is readily available in many of the foods that we eat, therefore it really isn't all that common to suffer from low potassium levels. The kidneys work to flush out excess potassium from the body. When the kidneys are not working properly they become inefficient at removing excess potassium. This leads to a buildup of potassium called hyperkalemia. Mild hyperkalemia can cause symptoms such as fatigue and nausea. When left untreated, severe hyperklalemia can lead to cardiac issues including cardiac arrest. For this reason, it is extremely important to have your potassium levels monitored on a regular basis by your medical provider. Unless you are undergoing dialysis to help rid excess potassium from your system, a wise course of action is to be watchful of the amount of potassium that you include in your diet. Some popular high potassium foods include bananas, avocados, oranges, artichokes, spinach, milk and some seasonings.

Dietary and Lifestyle Adjustments

When you embark on any dietary or lifestyle changes, there are bound to be some challenges along the way. This is just the way that it is when changes occur, regardless of whether those changes are positive or dreaded. Sometimes, you might be choosing to make changes to live a healthier lifestyle of your own initiative. When this happens, you are usually filled with enthusiasm. But, what happens when those changes are dictated by someone else or when you are told you must make these changes in order to protect your health, and possibly your life? Suddenly the stakes just became much higher and you can be enthusiastic on one hand, and possibly a little resentful on the other. This is a very normal response; however it is important to keep the end goal in mind.

You are the one in charge of your health, and when you commit to eating a way that nourishes your body and limits stress on your kidneys you are doing a great service towards your quality of life for years to come. You might view a renal diet plan as restrictive, but in fact the opposite is true. The renal diet plan is nutritious, delicious, and healthy and reduces the possibility of future restrictions in your life. Following any diet is about more than just the foods you choose to eat. It is about learning to incorporate your new dietary lifestyle into all aspects of your life. Here, we give you some tips to help you transition into a renal diet lifestyle successful and even enjoy it along the way.

Tell the people in your life about your new dietary plan. This includes family members, friends and possibly even coworkers. This doesn't mean that you need to hold a big meeting and hand out notes, however just mentioning it casually is likely to elicit questions and interest. The more the people in your life know about your dietary considerations, the more supportive they can be, which is especially important when it comes to gatherings, celebrations, holidays, etc.

Make a commitment to get and stay healthy. Try a new, or revisit a favorite exercise program, join a support group, find an accountability partner and set some goals for yourself. Being a healthy weight is very important in general, but it becomes even more important when you have underlying health concerns, such as kidney disease. Try setting goals that are challenging, but also realistic and achievable. Most people find that smaller goals can be more encouraging than large ones, so start by telling yourself that you are going to lose five pounds this month, or that you are going to go on four twenty minute walks this week. When you achieve one of your goals, give yourself credit. It was a challenge and you achieved it.

Take some steps to eliminate or reduce the emotional stress. Making changes, especially when those changes include coping with disease or bodily disharmony can really take a toll on your emotional state of mind. It is important to make taking care of your emotional health just as important as taking care of your physical health. You can begin by learning how to de-stress. This can be a highly individualized process, so take some time and really consider the best approach for you. You might want to try journaling, meditation, yoga, taking up a new hobby, finding a friend that you can talk to uncensored about everything that you are feeling or seeking professional therapy. Taking these steps in the beginning of the process can go a long way in preserving your emotional health later down the road.

Evaluate your bad habits and make an effort to quit. If you smoke, talk to your medical care provider about treatments to help you quit, restrict alcohol consumption, eliminate any drugs or medications that are nonessential and not prescribed by your doctor. The more you can eliminate, the less stress there will be on your kidneys.

Take all of your medications. Your medications have been prescribed for a reason and it is very important to follow your prescribed treatment plan. If you feel that some of your medications may be unnecessary, speak with your doctor about options. If you feel that you are not being listened to and your opinions are disregarded, then perhaps it is time to seek out a care provider that is more in line with your thoughts on the treatment and management of your condition. You might also wish to seek natural health care advice, but you should do so with the agreement of your primary physician.

Keep an eye on your blood pressure. This number is generally easy to monitor and it can be an important indicator of what is going on with your body as it can fluctuate with your diet, level of activity and the way that you are handling the stress in your life.

Turn grocery shopping into an adventure to get excited about it. Look for new recipes, including the ones in this book, and try meal planning. Now is a great time to get a little adventurous with flavors and foods that you might not be that familiar with. Experiment with new combinations of ingredients, or healthier adaptations of some of your favorites.

Always choose fresh over processed. Processed foods almost always contain an excessive amount of sodium and other bad stuff that you and your kidneys do not need.

Become a label reader. It is easy to take some things for granted, especially when it comes to the nutritional content of your favorite foods. Once you begin reading labels, you might be surprised at how much you didn't previously know about what exactly is in the food that you eat. Reading labels will also help you keep track of all of your key nutrient levels.

Keep a quick guideline of what you can and can't have on you at all times. This should include recommendations from your doctor, along with a list of some of the most important foods for you to avoid and the ones that you can eat freely. This is a handy reference, especially as you are settling into the renal diet lifestyle. Later, this can also serve as a quick reference to those around you.

Phone ahead before you eat out. This includes both restaurants and meals that you have been invited to enjoy in someone's home. It can be very frustrating to look forward to a meal out, only to arrive and find that there is nothing that you can eat without jeopardizing your health. When it comes to the foods that you shouldn't have, it simply isn't worth it to indulge and then suffer the consequences. Protecting your kidney health is on a whole other level than binging a little on your weight loss diet. Most restaurants will be able to make accommodations, especially if you have notified them ahead of time. Those restaurants that won't simply don't deserve your money anyway. Any host will want to make sure that all of their guests are able to enjoy themselves as much as possible and that includes making sure there is food and beverages for all of their guests to enjoy, including you.

Guidelines

Following a renal diet for your kidney health might seem a little overwhelming at first. Keeping track of how much phosphorus, calcium, potassium and protein each food has and realizing that while one food might be acceptable in one category, its level of another category turns it into a food that should be avoided, can feel complicated. Adapting to any new diet takes some adjustments and learning, however the renal diet does not need to be as complicated as it initially seems.

Here in this section we have set out some brief guidelines to help simplify the process for you. When reading through this section, it is important to remember that each person, each body and each condition are highly individualized. For that reason, the first source of your information and dietary guidelines should be your doctor. Here, we use a general approach to renal diet guidelines that can then be adapted to suit your individual needs.

Foods: What to Have and What to Avoid

Foods to Avoid:

• Whole grain starches such as whole grain cereal, quick cooking oats, bran muffins, wheat pasta and salted crackers or pretzels
• Deli sandwich meat
• Meat that is canned or smoked
• Processed cheese
• Vegetables such as artichokes, Brussels sprouts, potatoes, sweet potatoes, dark leafy greens such as spinach, okra, winter squash and beets
• Fruits such as avocados, tomatoes, bananas, apricots, tangerines, oranges, dried fruits, dates, honeydew melon
• Unhealthy fats
• Processed foods

• Alcohol and sodas, especially dark colored drinks

Foods to Enjoy:

• Non whole grain starches such as white rice, couscous, white bread, flour tortillas, pasta, unsalted crackers and popcorn.

• Vegetables such as green beans, cabbage, carrots, onions, lettuce, mushrooms, celery, zucchini and summer squash.

• Fruits such as apples, grapes, blueberries, cranberries, strawberries, and pears.

• Limited amounts of low fat dairy and some dairy substitutes

• Limited amounts of lean, quality protein. Limit consumption to no more than two to three ounces per meal.

• Healthy fats such as olive oil in moderation

What About Water?

You obviously need water to live, but drinking too much can be taxing for your kidneys and contribute to fluid retention. Speak with your doctor about fluid intake guidelines for your condition. It is also important to realize that any drink that you consume is meant to count toward your fluid intake. Additionally, foods such as frozen ices, soups and some fruits are going to contribute to your fluid intake as well. It is very important to keep quality of your water and fluid sources in mind. Avoid sodas because they can be high in phosphorus and sodium. Drink naturally flavored or unflavored waters, lemonade or teas instead. You will also want to invest in a water purifier, even if you have good quality drinking water in the community that you live in. Excess minerals and impurities can easily sneak into your water and cause your kidneys to work unnecessarily hard. Also, many bottles waters contain minerals, so always check the label before enjoying.

Other Considerations

If you need to lose weight, make sure that you do it under the supervision of your doctor. The logical approach might be to simply reduce your caloric intake. However, people with kidney conditions have other dietary concerns, including nutrient absorption issues, which might require additional calories to meet your nutritional needs.

You might need nutritional supplementation, however make sure that it is a supplement that your doctor either recommends or prescribes.

Talk to your doctor about your individual amounts of calories, protein, phosphorus, potassium and calcium that you should consume each day. Do not rely on internet sources of the advice of non medical professionals when it comes to your intake of each of these. It might take some time, especially if you are new to eating for kidney health, to know which foods are the best for your diet and which choices are a little high in some of the nutrients that you need to watch out for. You should keep a food journal that includes all foods, ingredients and levels of key nutrients to help you analyze and adjust your diet to your needs.

Try to avoid becoming thirsty. You are more likely to over consume liquids when you are suffering from thirst. To avoid this, sip on liquids throughout the day, avoid sodium and keep yourself cool on hot days.

The 30-day program included in this book does not take into consideration individual caloric needs. You will find that the three meals included will not satisfy the calorie needs of most people. The plan was formulated in this way to allow for several snacks throughout the day, or larger portion sizes when appropriate.

The 30 Day Meal Plan

In this chapter we have outlined a suggested 30 day meal plan. Keep in mind that your individual needs might be different and you might have to make adaptations along the way for your condition or individual tastes. It is acceptable to substitute one meal for another in the meal plan as long as you are aware of the key nutrients and keep them in balance. For example, there is generally one meal each day that is a little higher in protein. If you decide to substitute out a meal, make sure that you do not consume three higher protein meals in one day.

Meal suggestions that are in bold print have a recipe included in the next section. Additionally, your caloric intake might dictate larger portion sizes or more snacks throughout the day. Once again, I suggest keeping a food journal, especially in the beginning. Speaking of snacks, most people feel most satisfied and put less stress on their bodies when they consume three meals and several snacks each day. Some great snack ideas include:

• Unsalted, unbuttered popcorn
• Unsalted crackers
• Unsalted pretzels
• Animal Crackers
• Bagels
• Breadsticks
• Plain Rice Cakes
• Any fruit or vegetable on the approved foods list with a small amount of sour cream based dip

Day One

Breakfast: **Summer Vegetable Omelet**

Lunch: **Cajun Shrimp Salad**

Dinner: 2 ounce Pork Chop and Sautéed Apples

Day Two

Breakfast: **Red Pepper Strata**

Lunch: **Cranberry and Turkey Sandwich**

Dinner: **Gingery Eastern Lettuce Wraps**

Day Three

Breakfast: **Spicy Breakfast Burrito**

Lunch: **Cranberry Apple Salad**

Dinner: **Spicy Beef and Rice**

Day Four

Breakfast: Hardboiled Egg with White Toast and Berry Mix

Lunch: Shrimp Quesadilla

Dinner: **Lemon Caper Pasta**

Day Five

Breakfast: **No Fuss Pancakes**

Lunch: **Curry Chicken Salad** with White Roll

Dinner: **Cabbage Soup**

Day Six

Breakfast: Fruit Bowl and White Toast

Lunch: **Chicken Waldorf Salad**

Dinner: Turkey Sausage with Cabbage and Apples

Day Seven

Breakfast: **Huevos Rancheros**

Lunch: **Island Rice Salad**

Dinner: **Stuffed Chicken Breast**

Day Eight

Breakfast: Egg in a Hole with white bread

Lunch: 1.5 ounces of chicken with light dressing
in white pita with lettuce and choice vegetables

Dinner: Turkey Tacos

Day Nine

Breakfast: **Apple and Brie Omelet**

Lunch: Two Ounce Turkey Burger, green salad

Dinner: Extra Veggie Chef Salad

Day Ten

Breakfast: Spring Vegetable Tortilla

Lunch: **Taco Wrap**

Dinner: **Creamy Mushroom Risotto**

Day Eleven

Breakfast: Ground turkey patty on white English Muffin and Fruit

Lunch: Garden Salad with Tarragon Vinaigrette

Dinner: **Chicken Curry with Apples**

Day Twelve

Breakfast: **Zucchini Egg Cups**

Lunch: **Cajun Shrimp Salad**

Dinner: Baked Spaghetti Squash

Day Thirteen

Breakfast: **No Fuss Pancakes**

Lunch: **Taco Wrap**

Dinner: Herbed Pasta with Green Beans

Day Fourteen

Breakfast: Brie and Fruit Plate

Lunch: **Island Rice Salad**

Dinner: **Spicy Beef and Rice**

Day Fifteen

Breakfast: **Spicy Breakfast Burrito**

Lunch: Vegetable Pita

Dinner: Pork Chop with Sautéed Apples

Day Sixteen

Breakfast: Scrambled Egg Whites and Vegetables

Lunch: **Curry Chicken Salad** on White Roll

Dinner: **Cabbage Soup**

Day Seventeen

Breakfast: **Red Pepper Strata**

Lunch: **Chicken Waldorf Salad**

Dinner: **Creamy Mushroom Risotto**

Day Eighteen

Breakfast: Hardboiled Egg with Sautéed Red Peppers and Onions, Toast

Lunch: 2 ounces of Turkey Burger with Garden Salad

Dinner: **Gingery Eastern Lettuce Wraps**

Day Nineteen

Breakfast: **Spicy Breakfast Burrito**

Lunch: **Cranberry Apple Salad**

Dinner: **Lemon Caper Pasta**

Day Twenty

Breakfast: **Apple and Brie Omelet**

Lunch: Shrimp Quesadilla

Dinner: **Cabbage Soup**

Day Twenty One

Breakfast: **Huevos Rancheros**

Lunch: 2 ounces of turkey, 1 ounce brie, blueberries

Dinner: Turkey Sausage with Cabbage and Apples

Day Twenty Two

Breakfast: Fruit Bowl with White English Muffin and Honey

Lunch: **Cranberry Turkey Sandwich**

Dinner: **Stuffed Chicken Breasts**

Day Twenty Three

Breakfast: Spring Vegetable Tortilla

Lunch: **Taco Wrap**

Dinner: **Gingery Eastern Lettuce Wraps**

Day Twenty Four

Breakfast: **No Fuss Pancakes, Fruit**

Lunch: Egg White Salad Sandwich

Dinner: Shrimp and Pineapple Quesadilla

Day Twenty Five

Breakfast: **Zucchini Egg Cups**

Lunch: Turkey and Chicken Pinwheel Sandwiches

Dinner: Extra Veggie Chef Salad

Day Twenty Six

Breakfast: Eggs in a Hole with white bread

Lunch: **Cabbage Soup**

Dinner: **Stuffed Chicken Breast**

Day Twenty Seven

Breakfast: **Summer Vegetable Omelet**

Lunch: **Island Rice Salad**

Dinner: Dirty Rice with Shrimp

Day Twenty Eight

Breakfast: Brie and Fruit Plate

Lunch: Egg Drop Soup

Dinner: **Lemon Caper Pasta**

Day Twenty Nine

Breakfast: Ground Turkey with corn on white tortilla, Fruit

Lunch: **Cranberry Apple Salad**

Dinner: Herbed Pasta with Green Beans

Day Thirty

Breakfast: **No Fuss Pancakes**

Lunch: **Cajun Shrimp Salad**

Dinner: **Chicken Curry with Apples**

Kidney Friendly
**BREAKFAST
RECIPES**

Summer Vegetable Omelet

Serves: 2

Ingredients:
1 teaspoon olive oil
¼ cup onion, diced
¼ cup green bell pepper, diced
¼ cup zucchini, shredded
4 egg whites
¼ cup rice milk
1 tablespoon fresh chives

Directions:
Heat the olive oil in a skillet over medium heat.

Add in the onion and green bell pepper. Sauté until tender.

Add in the zucchini and sauté for 3-5 minutes, until tender and just beginning to brown.

Remove the vegetables from the skillet and set aside.

In a bowl, combine the egg whites, rice milk and chives.

Reduce the heat in the skillet to medium low and pour in the egg mixture.

Once the edges begin to firm, add the vegetable mixture to the center of the eggs and fold the edges over gently. Cook for 1-2 minutes.

Gently flip the omelet over and continue to cook until the desired firmness is reached.

Nutritional Information: Calories 88.0, Total Fat 2.8 g, Sodium 122.6 mg, Potassium 92.8 mg, Total Carbohydrate 8.3 g, Protein 8.0 g, Calcium 1.1 %, Phosphorus 1.6 %

Red Pepper Strata

Serves: 8

Ingredients:

3 cups sourdough bread, cubed

1 tablespoon olive oil

½ cup onion, diced

1 ½ cup red bell pepper, roasted and diced

1 cup mushrooms, sliced

4 eggs

3 egg whites

½ cup rice milk

¼ cup heavy cream

½ cup brie, cubed

1 tablespoon fresh tarragon

¼ cup fresh parsley, chopped

Directions:

Preheat the oven to 225°F.

Line a baking sheet with aluminum foil and
spread the cubed sourdough bread out onto the

baking sheet. Place the baking sheet in the oven and bake for 10-15 minutes, tossing once, until nicely toasted. Remove the toasted bread cubes from the oven and set aside to cool.

Meanwhile, add the olive oil to a skillet over medium heat. Add in the onions and mushrooms and sauté for 3-4 minutes. Add in the red bell pepper and set aside.

Lightly oil an 8x8 baking dish. Spread one half of the bread cubes into the baking dish, topped with one half of the vegetables. Repeat until all of the bread cubes and vegetables have been used.

Next, combine the eggs, egg whites, rice milk, heavy cream, tarragon and parsley in a bowl. Whisk until well blended.

Pour the egg mixture over the bread and vegetables, tapping lightly to make sure the egg mixture goes all of the way to the bottom, completely saturating all of the bread.

Sprinkle the brie cheese over the top.

Cover and refrigerate for at least two hours or overnight.

Remove the strata from the refrigerator and bring to room temperature for at least 15 minutes while preheating the oven to 325°F.

Place the pan in the oven and bake for 45-50 minutes, or until set in the center.
Cut and serve.

Nutritional Information: Calories 193.9, Total Fat 9.7 g, Sodium 268.7 mg, Potassium 180.0 mg, Total Carbohydrate 17.5 g, Protein 9.3 g, Calcium 5.6 %, Phosphorus 11.2 %

No Fuss Pancakes

Serves: 10

Ingredients:

2 cups all purpose white flour

1 teaspoon baking soda

¼ teaspoon salt

1 tablespoon sugar

2 eggs

1 ½ tablespoon vegetable oil

2 cups low fat milk

1 tablespoon vinegar

1 teaspoon vanilla extract

1 teaspoon ground nutmeg

1 cup blueberries, optional

Directions:

Combine the milk and vinegar in a small bowl.
Stir and set aside for several minutes.

Sift together the flour, baking soda, salt and sugar in a bowl.

Place the eggs in a separate large bowl and whisk until creamy.

Combine the eggs with vegetable oil and milk mixture. Whisk or beat until well blended.

Next, add in the vanilla and nutmeg. Stir well. Add the dry ingredients to the wet ingredients, working in small increments until blended.

Lightly oil a griddle or frying pan over medium to medium high heat. Pour about ¼ cup of the mixture onto the griddle and cook until bubbles begin to form on the top.

If using blueberries, sprinkle them on top of the pancakes at this point.

Using a spatula, carefully flip the pancakes over and cook for an additional 1-2 minutes.

Remove from the griddle and keep warm until ready to serve.

Nutritional Information: Calories 151.3, Total Fat 3.3 g, Sodium 177.5 mg, Potassium 129.9 mg, Total Carbohydrate 24.5 g, Protein 5.6 g, Calcium 6.9%, Phosphorus 9.8%

Huevos Rancheros

Serves: 2

Ingredients:

1 tablespoon olive oil

1 cup asparagus, chopped

½ cup onion, sliced

2 teaspoons cayenne pepper sauce

1 teaspoon lemon juice

2 teaspoons crushed red pepper flakes

2 eggs

2 corn tortillas

¼ cup shredded Mexican cheese

Directions:

Lightly brush a skillet with olive oil and heat over medium to medium high heat.

Add the tortillas and cook until nicely toasted, flipping once.

Add the remaining oil to the skillet and reduce the heat to medium.

Add in the onions and asparagus. Season the vegetables with cayenne pepper sauce, lemon juice and crushed red pepper flakes. Sauté for 5-7 minutes or until the vegetables are crisp tender.

Remove the vegetables from the skillet and add them to the toasted tortillas.

Next, add the eggs to the skillet and cooked to desired doneness.

Place the eggs on top of the vegetables. Sprinkle with shredded Mexican cheese before serving.

Nutritional Information: Calories 285.4, Total Fat 17.2 g, Sodium 195.7 mg, Potassium 322.1 mg, Total Carbohydrate 21.7 g, Protein 12.3 g, Calcium 13.4%, Phosphorus 21.3%

Spicy Breakfast Burrito

Serves: 2

Ingredients:

2 medium sized flour tortillas

4 eggs

2 teaspoons olive oil

½ cup poblano pepper, diced

¼ cup red onion, diced

1 teaspoon ground cumin

½ teaspoon ground cayenne

½ teaspoon coarse ground black pepper

Directions:

Place the eggs in a bowl and whisk until blended. Set aside.

Heat the olive oil in a skillet over medium heat.

Add the poblano pepper and red onion to the skillet.

Season the vegetables with the cumin, cayenne and black pepper. Sauté until the onions and peppers are tender.

Reduce the heat to medium low and add in the egg.

Cook, while scrambling, until the eggs are cooked to preferred doneness. Serve in warmed flour tortillas.

Nutritional Information: Calories 293.1, Total Fat 15.4 g, Sodium 295.6 mg, Potassium 211.3 mg, Total Carbohydrate 20.3 g, Protein 15.6 g, Calcium 5.6%, Phosphorus 24.7%

Apple and Brie Omelet

Serves: 2

Ingredients:

2 eggs

2 egg whites

1 tablespoon butter

¼ cup sweet yellow onion, diced

1 cup apple, peeled and sliced

2 teaspoons fresh tarragon, chopped

¼ cup brie, cubed

Directions:

Melt the butter in a skillet over medium heat.

Add the onion and apples. Season with the fresh tarragon and sauté until crisp tender or desired texture. Remove the apples and onions from the skillet and set aside.

Combine the eggs and the egg whites in a bowl and whisk until well blended and creamy.

Reduce the heat of the skillet to medium low.

Pour the egg mixture into the skillet and cook until the edges begin to firm.

Add the apple and onion mixture to the center of the omelet.

Gently lift the edges of the omelet and fold over into a half moon shape.

Sprinkle the brie over the top of the omelet and cook until set in the center.

Nutritional Information: Calories 240.1, Total Fat 15.8 g, Sodium 240.6 mg, Potassium 196.6 mg, Total Carbohydrate 11.1 g, Protein 14.1 g, Calcium 6.3%, Phosphorus 14.7%

Zucchini Egg Cups

Serves: 3

Ingredients:

3 eggs

3 egg whites

¼ cup scallions, sliced

1 cup zucchini, shredded with excess moisture removed

¼ cup fresh parsley, chopped

1 clove garlic, crushed and minced

1 tablespoon fresh grated parmesan cheese

Directions:

Preheat the oven to 350°F and coat 6 regular sized muffin tins with a non stick cooking spray.

In a bowl, combine the eggs and the egg whites. Whisk until blended and creamy.

In another bowl, combine the scallions, zucchini, parsley, garlic and parmesan cheese.

Mix well. Transfer equal amounts of the vegetable mixture into each of the muffin tins.
Pour the egg mixture into each and then tap the pan gently to make sure the egg mixture settles to the bottom.

Place the tin in the oven and bake for 30 minutes, or until set in the center.

Nutritional Information: Calories 113.4, Total Fat 5.5 g, Sodium 162.9 mg, Potassium 317.2 mg, Total Carbohydrate 4.7 g, Protein 11.4 g, Calcium 6.5%, Phosphorus 15.1%

Kidney Friendly
LUNCH
RECIPES

Cajun Shrimp Salad

Serves: 4

Ingredients:

4 cups lettuce, torn

1 cup cucumber, sliced

1 cup radish, sliced

¼ cup red onion, diced

2 cloves garlic, crushed and minced

½ cup low fat sour cream

1 teaspoon lime juice

1 tablespoon fresh cilantro, chopped

½ lb. shrimp, cleaned and deveined

2 teaspoons olive oil

1 teaspoon Cajun spices

½ teaspoon cayenne powder

½ teaspoon coarse ground black pepper

Directions:

Place the lettuce, cucumber, radish and red onion in a large bowl. Toss to mix.

In a separate bowl, combine the low fat sour cream, lime juice and cilantro. Whisk until well blended.

Add the dressing to the salad and toss to coat. Set aside.

Heat the olive oil in a skillet over medium heat.

Add the shrimp and season with the Cajun spices, cayenne powder and black pepper.

Cook for 2-4 minutes, stirring frequently, until no longer pink.

Remove the shrimp from the heat, slice if desired and add directly to the salad. Serve immediately.

(If you prefer a chilled salad, allow the shrimp to cool before adding them to the vegetables. Cover and refrigerate.)

Nutritional Information: Calories 134.3, Total Fat 6.2 g, Sodium 157.4 mg, Potassium 354.2 mg, Total Carbohydrate 6.0 g, Protein 13.8 g, Calcium 8.0%, Phosphorus 13.6%

Cranberry Apple Salad

Serves: 4

Ingredients:

4 cups lettuce, chopped

2 cups apples, peeled and diced

1 tablespoon shallots

1 cup cranberries

1 teaspoon white sugar

2 teaspoons butter or olive oil

¼ cup water

1 tablespoon balsamic vinegar

Directions:

Sprinkle the apples with lemon juice, if desired, to prevent browning.

Combine the lettuce and apples in a large bowl. Toss to mix.

Add the butter or olive oil to a skillet over medium heat.

Add in the shallots and cranberries. Sprinkle them with the white sugar and sauté for 3-4 minutes, or until the shallots are tender.

Add the water and balsamic vinegar. Cook, stirring frequently, until the liquid bubbles and reduces.

Remove the skillet from the heat and allow to cool slightly before adding to the salad.

Toss to mix and serve immediately.

Nutritional Information: Calories 73.9, Total Fat 2.0 g, Sodium 7.5 mg, Potassium 173.1 mg, Total Carbohydrate 15.2 g, Protein 0.8 g, Calcium 1.7%, Phosphorus 2.0%

Chicken Curry Salad

Serves: 4

Ingredients:

1 ½ cup cooked chicken, cubed or shredded

¼ cup red onion, diced

2 teaspoons olive oil

1 tablespoon curry spice

½ cup celery, diced

1 cup apples, peeled and diced

¼ cup light mayonnaise

½ teaspoon coriander

1 teaspoon coarse ground black pepper

Directions:

Heat the olive oil in a skillet over medium heat.

Add the shallots and sauté until tender.

Add in the chicken and season the mixture with the curry spices. Cook for 1-2 minutes, and then remove from heat and allow to cool.

Once the chicken has cooled, transfer it to a bowl and combine it with the celery, apples, mayonnaise, coriander and black pepper. Toss to mix.

Serve immediately or cover and refrigerate until ready to serve.

Nutritional Information: Calories 115.2, Total Fat 5.2 g, Cholesterol 26.3 mg, Sodium 107.3 mg, Potassium 177.7 mg, Total Carbohydrate 7.2 g, Protein 10.0 g, Calcium 1.5%, Phosphorus 9.3%

Chicken Waldorff Salad

Serves: 4

Ingredients:

½ lb. chicken, cooked and cubed

1 cup green apples, chopped

1 cup red apple, chopped

½ cup grapes, quartered

1 cup celery, cubed

¼ cup sweet yellow onion, diced

¼ cup low fat mayonnaise

1 tablespoon cranberry juice

Directions:

Combine the chicken, green apples, red apples, grapes, celery and onions in a bowl. Toss to mix.

In a separate small bowl, combine the mayonnaise and cranberry juice. Whisk together until well blended.

Add the dressing to the salad and toss to coat.

Cover tightly and refrigerate at least 1 hour before serving.

Nutritional Information: Calories 145.5, Total Fat 4.3 g, Sodium 151.1 mg, Potassium 299.9 mg, Total Carbohydrate 13.8 g, Protein 13.4 g, Calcium 2.7%, Phosphorus 12.9%

Island Rice Salad

Serves: 6

Ingredients:

4 cups white rice, cooked

½ lb. shrimp, cooked and sliced

1 cup jicama, sliced into matchsticks and then chopped

1 cup pineapple, diced

½ cup red onion, diced

½ cup red bell pepper, diced

¼ cup fresh cilantro, chopped

¼ cup low fat sour cream

2 tablespoons white wine vinegar

1 tablespoon fresh chives, chopped

Directions:

In a bowl, combine the cooked rice, cooked shrimp, jicama, pineapple, red onion, red bell pepper and cilantro. Toss to mix.

In a separate small bowl, combine the sour cream, white wine and fresh chives. Whisk together until well blended.

Add the dressing mixture to the salad and mix together.

Serve immediately, or cover and refrigerate until ready to serve.

Nutritional Information: Calories 237.5, Total Fat 1.8 g, Sodium 89.4 mg, Potassium 212.5 mg, Total Carbohydrate 42.8 g, Protein 11.6 g, Calcium 3.2%, Phosphorus 11.2%

Tarragon Vinaigrette

Serves: 8

Ingredients:

¼ cup olive oil

2 teaspoons shallots, minced

2 tablespoons Dijon mustard

2 tablespoons apple cider vinegar

2 tablespoons fresh tarragon

1 teaspoon coarse ground black pepper

Directions:

Combine all ingredients and whisk together until blended and lightly emulsified.

Transfer to a jar, cover and refrigerate until ready to use.

Nutritional Information: Calories 64.2, Total Fat 7.0 g, Sodium 90.1 mg, Potassium 10.8 mg, Total Carbohydrate 0.1 g, Protein 0.0 g, Calcium 0.0%, Phosphorus 0.0%

Cranberry and Turkey Sandwich

Serves: 4

Ingredients:

½ lb. cooked turkey (non deli meat)

2 teaspoons olive oil

¼ cup red onion

½ cup cranberries

¼ cup apple juice

¼ cup water

1 teaspoon white sugar

1 tablespoon fresh thyme

Lettuce for serving

White bread for serving (not included in nutritional content)

Directions:

Heat the olive oil in a saucepan over medium heat.

Add the onions and sauté until translucent.

Add in the cranberries, apple juice, sugar and water. Bring the liquid to a low boil, then reduce the heat and let simmer for 15 minutes, or until the cranberries have softened.

Remove the saucepan from the heat and transfer the contents, along with the thyme, to a blender. Pulse briefly, just enough to break down the cranberries.

Spread the cranberry sauce on bread, add the turkey and lettuce before serving.

Nutritional Information: Calories 51.2, Total Fat 2.3 g, Sodium 9.9 mg, Potassium 70.4 mg, Total Carbohydrate 3.4 g, Protein 4.5 g, Calcium 0.6 %, Phosphorus 3.7 %

Taco Wrap

Serves: 4

Ingredients:

½ lb. lean ground beef

¼ cup canned green chilies

2 cloves garlic, crushed and minced

1 teaspoon smoked chili powder

1 teaspoon cayenne powder

1 cup red bell pepper, diced

½ cup red onion, diced

¼ cup fresh cilantro, chopped

2 teaspoons vinegar

Flour tortillas for serving

Directions:

Place the ground beef in a skillet over medium heat. Cook until browned and drain off any excess grease.

Add in the green chilies, garlic, chili powder and cayenne powder. Stir and cook an additional 3-4 minutes.

Combine the red bell pepper, red onion, cilantro and vinegar together and mix well.

Transfer the meat mixture to the flour tortillas. Top with the vegetable mixture and roll tightly before serving.

Nutritional Information: Calories 271.7, Total Fat 11.1 g, Sodium 239.1 mg, Potassium 390.8 mg, Total Carbohydrate 22.8 g, Protein 19.3 g, Calcium 3.0%,Phosphorus 13.7%

Cabbage Soup

Serves: 6

Ingredients:

6 cups low sodium or homemade vegetable stock

½ lb. boneless skinless chicken breast, cubed

2 tablespoons olive oil

1 cup yellow onion, sliced

2 cups zucchini, sliced

4 cups cabbage, shredded

1 teaspoon coriander

1 teaspoon turmeric

½ teaspoon cinnamon

1 teaspoon black pepper

Cooked white rice for serving (optional)

Directions:

Heat the olive oil in a large soup pot.

Add in the chicken and sauté until browned.
Remove from the pot and set aside.

Add the onion to the pot and sauté for 2-3 minutes.

Next, add the cabbage and season with the coriander, turmeric, cinnamon and black pepper. Cook for 4-5 minutes.

Add the chicken back into the pot, along with the zucchini.

Add in the vegetable stock and bring the soup to a boil over medium high heat.

Once the liquid boils, reduce the heat to low and simmer for 20 minutes, or until the chicken is cooked through.

Serve with cooked rice, if desired.

Nutritional Information: Calories 135.3, Total Fat 5.9 g, Potassium 410.4 mg, Total Carbohydrate 10.9 g, Protein 10.1 g, Calcium 6.5%, Phosphorus 12.0%

Kidney Friendly
DINNER
RECIPES

Gingery Eastern Lettuce Wraps

Serves: 6

Ingredients:

1 cup cucumber, peeled and diced

1 cup red bell pepper, diced

2 cups cabbage, shredded and chopped

½ cup scallions, sliced

2 tablespoons rice vinegar

½ teaspoon white sugar

1 lb. ground turkey

1 tablespoon garlic chili paste

¼ cup low sodium soy sauce

3 cloves garlic, crushed and minced

1 tablespoon fresh grated ginger

2 teaspoons sesame oil

2 cups cooked couscous

12 large lettuce leaves

Directions:

In a bowl, combine the cucumber, red bell pepper, cabbage and scallions.

Next, mix together the rice vinegar and rice sugar. Whisk until the sugar is completely dissolved. Add the dressing mixture to the vegetables and toss to coat.

Cover and place in the refrigerator for at least 1 hour.

In a bowl, combine the ground turkey, garlic chili paste, low sodium soy sauce, garlic, ginger and sesame oil. Mix well.

Place the meat mixture in a large skillet or frying pan and cook over medium heat until browned and cooked through.

Lay out the lettuce leave on a flat surface.

To each leaf add some of the cooked couscous, then the cooked meat mixture and finally, the chilled vegetables.

Roll each leaf tightly before serving.

Nutritional Information: Calories 210.2, Total Fat 7.2 g, Sodium 376.7 mg, Potassium 245.3 mg, Total Carbohydrate 18.5 g, Protein 18.4 g, Calcium 3.3%, Phosphorus 3.9%

Spicy Beef and Vegetables

Serves: 8

Ingredients:

1 lb. lean beef, sliced thinly

1 teaspoon black pepper

½ teaspoon cardamom

1 cup onions, sliced

1 cup celery, diced

1 cup green bell peppers, sliced

1 cup carrots, shredded

1 tablespoon jalapeno pepper, diced

4 cloves garlic, crushed and minced

2 tablespoons olive oil

1 tablespoon garlic chili paste

2 teaspoons crushed red pepper flakes

¼ cup low sodium soy sauce

1 tablespoon rice vinegar

2 teaspoons sesame oil

6 cups cooked white rice

Directions:

Add the olive oil to a skillet over medium heat.

Season the beef with black pepper and cardamom. Add the meat to the skillet and cook until browned. Remove from the skillet and set aside.

To the still warm skillet, add the onions, celery and green bell peppers. Cook, stirring frequently for approximately 5 minutes, or until the vegetables become crisp tender.

Add the carrots, jalapeno pepper and garlic to the skillet. Cook for an additional 2-3 minutes.

Combine the garlic chili paste, crushed red pepper flakes, soy sauce, rice vinegar and sesame oil together. Whisk until well blended.

Add the meat back into the skillet with the vegetables and then pour the sauce into the pan.

Cook, stirring frequently until heated through and the sauce thickens slightly. Serve over cooked rice.

Nutritional Information: Calories 321.0, Total Fat 7.3 g, Sodium 283.7 mg, Potassium 400.5 mg, Protein 17.3 g, Calcium 2.1%, Phosphorus 18.9%

Lemon Caper Pasta

Serves: 4

Ingredients:

4 cups cooked angel hair pasta

2 tablespoons olive oil

4 cloves garlic, crushed and minced

2 tablespoons capers

2 tablespoons lemon juice

1 teaspoon lemon zest

1 tablespoon fresh tarragon

1 teaspoon coarse ground black pepper

¼ cup fresh parsley, chopped

2 tablespoons freshly grated parmesan

Directions:

Add the olive oil to a skillet over medium heat.

Add the garlic to the skillet and sauté for 1-2 minutes.

Next add in the capers, lemon juice, lemon zest, tarragon, and black pepper. Cook for 1-2 minute.

Add the cooked pasta to the skillet and toss to coat. Cook just until warmed through.

Serve garnished with parsley and a bit of fresh parmesan.

Nutritional Information: Calories 277.9, Total Fat 8.8 g, Sodium 176.1 mg, Potassium 32.2 mg, Total Carbohydrate 43.5 g, Protein 8.4 g, Calcium 4.5%, Phosphorus 2.7%

Stuffed Chicken Breasts

Serves: 4

Ingredients:

4 – 3 ounce boneless, skinless chicken breast

1 tablespoon olive oil

¼ cup onion, chopped

2 cloves garlic, crushed and minced

¼ cup celery, chopped

1 cup mushrooms, sliced

1 teaspoon rubbed sage

2 cups couscous, cooked

¼ cup Dijon mustard

1 tablespoon pure maple syrup

1 tablespoon balsamic vinegar

Directions:

Butterfly each of the chicken breast, so that it can be opened up to insert the stuffing.

Preheat the oven to 350°F and line a small baking dish with aluminum foil.

Place the olive oil in a skillet over medium heat.

Add the onion, garlic and celery. Sauté for 3-5 minutes.

Add in the mushrooms and sage, and sauté for an additional 2 minutes.

Remove the skillet from the heat, add in the cooked couscous and set aside to cool slightly.

In a small bowl, whisk together the Dijon mustard, maple syrup and balsamic vinegar until blended.

Using a basting brush, spread a little of the mixture over both sides of the chicken breasts.

Spoon the filling mixture into the center of each chicken breast and fold over. Secure with wooden picks or cooking twine.

Place the skillet back over medium heat and add the chicken breasts. Cook until lightly browned on both sides.

Transfer the chicken breast the baking pan and pour over any remaining sauce.

Place in the oven and bake for 20 minutes, or until cooked through.

Nutritional Information: Calories 257.2, Total Fat 6.0 g, Sodium 417.3 mg, Potassium 320.9 mg, Protein 23.0 g, Calcium 2.5%, Phosphorus 20.4%

Creamy Mushroom Risotto

Serves: 6

Ingredients:

2 tablespoons butter

1 cup sweet yellow onion, diced

1 ½ cup Arborio rice

¼ cup dry white wine

2 cups portabello mushrooms, diced

1 teaspoon rubbed sage

1 teaspoon coarse ground black pepper

4 cups low sodium or homemade vegetable stock

1 bay leaf

1 sprig fresh rosemary

¼ cup freshly grated asiago cheese

Directions:

Place the vegetable stock, bay leave and rosemary sprig in a saucepan over medium heat. Allow the liquid to come to a near boil, then reduce to low and let simmer.

Add the butter to a large skillet over medium heat.

Add the yellow onion and sauté until tender.

Next, add in the Arborio rice and cook, stirring frequently, for 3-4 minutes or until lightly toasted.

Add in the white wine and cook, stirring frequently, until the wine reduces.

Add in 2 cups of the vegetable stock to the rice. Stir, while cooking, until the liquid begins to bubble. Cover and cook for 5 minutes.

Remove the cover, add in the mushrooms, sage, black pepper and 1 cup of the vegetable stock. Stir, cover and cook an additional 10 minutes.

Remove the cover and slowly ladle in the remaining stock, stirring constantly, until the rice becomes tender, approximately 5-7 minutes.

Add in the asiago cheese right before serving.

Nutritional Information: Calories 263.6, Total Fat 7.0 g, Sodium 199.4 mg, Potassium 124.2 mg, Total Carbohydrate 17.1 g, Protein 6.8 g, Calcium 2.1%, Phosphorus 3.1%

Curry Chicken with Apples

Serves: 6

Ingredients:

1 lb. boneless, skinless chicken breast, cut into strips

2 tablespoons olive oil

1 cup onion, chopped

2 cups apples, peeled and chopped

2 cloves garlic, crushed and minced

1 serrano pepper, finely diced

1 tablespoon curry powder

1 teaspoon cardamom

2 teaspoons fresh grated ginger

2 tablespoons flour

1 cup low sodium or homemade chicken stock

1 cup unflavored rice milk

½ cup pineapple, chopped

Fresh cilantro for garnish

Cooked white rice for serving, optional

Directions:

Preheat the oven to 350°F and lightly oil an 8x8 baking dish with cooking spray.

Place the chicken strips in the baking dish.

Add the olive oil to a large skillet over medium heat.

Add the onions, apples, garlic and serrano pepper. Sauté until highly fragrant, approximately 2-3 minutes.

Season the skillet with curry powder, cardamom and fresh grated ginger. Cook for an additional 1-2 minutes.

Sprinkle in the flour and toss to coat.

Add in the chicken stock and rice milk. Increase the heat to medium high and bring to a low boil. Stir and remove the sauce from the heat and allow to cool slightly.

Add the pineapple to the sauce and then pour the sauce over the chicken.

Place the baking dish in the oven and bake for approximately 30 minutes, or until the chicken is cooked through.

Nutritional Information: Calories 199.4, Total Fat 7.2 g, Sodium 158.1 mg, Potassium 303.6 mg, Total Carbohydrate 15.5 g, Protein 18.4 g, Calcium 2.3%, Phosphorus 16.3%

Conclusion

There really is nothing more important than your health. Without it, you cannot fully enjoy all of the other aspects of your life. It can be easy to become stressed, anxious and depressed when you are suffering from a chronic health condition, especially one that can potentially become as serious as renal failure. This book has been created to help you see the delicious part of life once again. Yes, your life is going to require some adjustments; however, there is no reason to dread them.

The renal diet does not need to be bland, dull or unexciting. Here, we have presented 30 days to you that show you that you have nothing to fear or dread. With any health condition, including kidney disease, you should be working hand in hand with your medical care provider to determine the best course of care for your unique condition. With the help of your care providers, the recipes in this book and your determined and encouraging attitude, renal failure can become less of an obstacle and you can once again take control of your life.

Made in the USA
Middletown, DE
18 December 2016